Stop Smoking

Unveil The Hidden Techniques To Effectively Cease The Persistent Desire For Smoking Cigarettes, Tobacco,

E-Cigarettes, And All Nicotine-Infused Products On A Permanent Basis

(The Enigmatic Phenomena That Will Divert Individuals

From The Practice Of Smoking)

Adnan Fleck

TABLE OF CONTENT

Start Quitting Today 1

Mitigating Or Alleviating Nicotine Dependency To Facilitate Smoking Cessation 6

Comprehensive Insights Into The Hazards Of Tobacco Smoke And The Necessity Of Smoking Cessation 13

The Global Menace of Tobacco Smoke 14

Your Progression Of Abstinence: First, Second, And Third Days 45

Timetable And Regimen 58

The Challenges Of Smoking Cessation: Understanding The Difficulty 65

Creating A Quit Plan 79

A Concise Chronological Account Of The Origins And Evolution Of Hypnosis 114

Bringing The Mind Back To Sobriety 130

Extracting Lessons From Prior Endeavors............157

Establishing A Consistent Respiratory Routine ...163

Ensuring The Continuation Of An Environment Free From Smoketo..166

Start Quitting Today

Include the content of this chapter, where you will gain insight on commencing the process of cessation starting from today. During the upcoming month, it is imperative for you to comprehend and implement the principles conveyed by the acronym START.

S: Establish a firm deadline for cessation. Please select a date within the range of 15 to 30 days from the present moment. In this manner, you will possess an ample amount of determination, resilience, and justification to cease the habit of smoking. By adopting this approach, you have the opportunity to enhance your inner fortitude. Gradually endeavor to abstain from one cigarette at a time.

T: Kindly inform your acquaintances, relatives, colleagues, and associates about your earnest commitment to cease smoking. It is imperative to inform all significant individuals in your life regarding your intended course of action. Kindly request their support and encouragement towards your plan, while also acknowledging that you anticipate moments of discouragement and a desire to give up. It is recommended that you seek assistance from them to provide encouragement during moments when you contemplate giving up your efforts. If you so desire, you may opt for a cessation companion. By doing so, you will not experience a sense of isolation throughout the procedure.

A: Foresee potential obstacles and make necessary arrangements to overcome them in advance while undertaking the cessation journey. The anticipation of experiencing nicotine withdrawal symptoms, such as a strong desire to smoke and challenges of both psychological and physiological nature, is advised. These are the prevailing challenges extensively encountered. Are you aware that a significant majority of individuals who have quit smoking tend to relapse within the subsequent three months? Avoid becoming a contributor to these failure statistics.

R: Elimination of cigarettes and any associated paraphernalia from your vehicle, professional environment, and domicile. Regardless of their cost or sentimental significance, cigarettes, matches, lighters, and even ashtrays should be discarded. Individuals with a noticeable odor of smoke should undergo a comprehensive cleaning process. If it is feasible, you might consider cleaning your vehicle, your floor coverings, as well as your furnishings.

T: Consult with a healthcare professional and seek any required support.

Physicians have the ability to aid individuals in their smoking cessation journey by prescribing the essential pharmaceutical treatments intended to facilitate their quitting efforts. This will moderately alleviate the symptoms of withdrawal. Medical professionals have the expertise to provide you with superior healthcare alternatives. You may also ask a pharmacist about the safest nicotine gum, nicotine lozenges, and nicotine patches.here...

Mitigating Or Alleviating Nicotine Dependency To Facilitate Smoking Cessation

The cessation strategy involves reducing smoking gradually in the period leading up to the designated quit date. It can be likened to traveling in the least congested lane of a highway, wherein you will still reach your destination, albeit potentially with a slightly swifter journey. If you are desirous of quitting smoking but not yet fully prepared to do so, adopting a gradual reduction strategy as a means to ultimately quit may appear suitable for your circumstances. As your designated quit date approaches, it is commendable that you are displaying initiative by reducing your consumption.

Based on empirical evidence, individuals who opt for a gradual reduction approach to quit smoking have comparable odds of success to those who abruptly cease smoking on their designated quit day. In order to ensure success, it is imperative that you establish a predetermined cutoff date prior to commencing the reduction of your intake.

Implementing a gradual reduction approach enables you to gradually reduce your tobacco consumption at a pace suitable to your preferences, thus alleviating any undue stress as you approach your designated cessation date.

What strategies can I employ to minimize my smoking habits and ultimately achieve cessation?

I would recommend considering the implementation of these techniques as a means to assist in ceasing the habit of smoking, particularly if you are contemplating the utilization of the reduction method as a means of quitting.

1. Establish your designated timeframe for quitting: Identify your predetermined period for cessation: Evaluate the specific duration within which you intend to quit:

Please select the duration during which you intend to allocate your efforts toward the attainment of your cessation date.

It appears that implementing a time frame of 2-4 weeks is the most efficacious approach in order to progressively diminish to minimal levels before completely ceasing.

2. Engage in diligent preparations and develop strategic arrangements:

▪ Avoid locations where you previously engaged in smoking.

Replace outdated smoking practices with fresh, engaging pastimes.

▪ Alter the behaviors associated with smoking that you currently possess

Utilize the funds that you conserve from ceasing tobacco usage to strategize enticing rewards.

Secure aid during your endeavor to quit smoking

Kindly seek the assistance of a close acquaintance or a family member to support your commitment in overcoming the habit of smoking.

▪ Register for an online smoking cessation program. Alternatively, consider perusing a post featuring uplifting sentiments shared by an individual who may similarly face challenges with tobacco cravings. Examine the strategies employed by individuals in effectively controlling their inclinations to engage in tobacco consumption.

3. Participating in physical activity can assist in mitigating the urge to smoke. Even short intervals of physical activity, such as repeatedly engaging in stair sprints, have the potential to alleviate the urge to smoke. Engage in outdoor physical activity through walking or jogging. Incorporate exercises such as squats, deep knee bends, pushups, sprinting in place, or utilizing a staircase for ascending and descending if you are at a location such as home or work. Might I suggest exploring alternative activities such as engaging in prayer, practicing the art of sewing, honing one's skills in woodworking, or indulging in the therapeutic practice of journaling, for those who find little enjoyment in physical exercise. Alternatively, one could engage in activities such as tidying or organizing documents to deflect one's focus.

Comprehensive Insights Into The Hazards Of Tobacco Smoke And The Necessity Of Smoking Cessation

The Global Menace of Tobacco Smoke

Tobacco use is the primary contributing factor to global mortality, morbidity, and economic inequality. Extensive research and empirical evidence confirm that tobacco consumption stands as the foremost cause of avoidable ailments and infirmities on a global scale. Additionally, it serves as the primary cause of premature mortality on a global scale. Tobacco claims the lives of nearly six million individuals annually. More than five million of these fatalities arise as a result of the direct utilization of tobacco products; specifically, over five million individuals who engage in smoking lose their lives on an annual basis. The remaining fatalities pertain to individuals who do not smoke - specifically, those who have been subjected to the inhalation of second-hand tobacco smoke. It might be unexpected to note that the prevalence of smokers is predominantly concentrated in low and middle income countries, despite the high cost associated with cigarettes.

The mortality rate resulting from smoke exposure is expected to increase significantly unless immediate and comprehensive actions are taken.

The Global Impact of Tobacco Smoking: Ramifications and Implications

Smoking stands as an eminent global menace to public health, owing to its substantial fatality toll. Tobacco smoke consists of more than 7000 chemical compounds. There is evidence to suggest that 250 of these chemicals possess harmful properties, while 69 have been definitively linked to the direct causation of cancer. In the 20th century, tobacco usage was responsible for a staggering number of fatalities, exceeding 100 million in total. If the prevalence of smoking does not decline, it is anticipated that tobacco will be responsible for causing one billion fatalities in the 21st century. This amounts to more than 8 million fatalities annually. A significant majority of fatalities will be witnessed in countries with low to moderate income levels.

The Impacts of Tobacco Smoke in Economically Disadvantaged Nations.

Approximately 80% of the global smoking population resides in countries with lower and middle-level incomes. The impact of tobacco-associated illnesses in these countries is profoundly destructive. The premature demise of individuals who smoke incurs financial losses for their families, while simultaneously leading to escalated healthcare costs and impeding economic progress.

To compound matters, it has been observed in select low to middle-income nations that households consent to the employment of children in the cultivation of tobacco, thereby exacerbating the situation. This is done to enable them to generate an income and thus contribute to enhancing the prosperity of the household. Therefore, these unfortunate children are being subjected to the peril of acquiring "green tobacco sickness", a medical condition stemming from the dermal absorption of nicotine through direct contact with moist tobacco foliage.

Tobacco: A Slow Killer

Tobacco is a lethargic destructor of life. This is attributed to the premise that individuals' health remains unaffected until a considerable span of years has elapsed subsequent to their initiation of smoking. It has been established that, currently, tobacco is responsible for the loss of roughly one life every six seconds. Specifically, smoking is responsible for the mortality of ten percent of the adult population. Approximately half of individuals who smoke will inevitably develop an illness associated with smoking and ultimately succumb to its effects.

In particular: Medical conditions that arise as a direct result of tobacco consumption

Tobacco smoking is associated with a multitude of deleterious health conditions. The specific diseases encompassed within this group consist of chronic obstructive pulmonary disease (COPD, which includes chronic bronchitis and emphysema), coronary heart disease, stroke, abdominal aortic aneurysm, acute myeloid leukemia, cataract, pneumonia, periodontitis, and cancers affecting the bladder, esophagus, larynx, lungs, oral cavity, throat, cervix, kidneys, stomach, and pancreas.

Additionally, tobacco use has been found to be interconnected with a range of other health issues and disorders, such as delayed wound healing, reduced fertility, and peptic ulcer disease.

Furthermore, should pregnant women engage in smoking or be exposed to second-hand smoke, there is a heightened likelihood of their infants being born with a low birth weight. Expectant mothers who smoke or are exposed to secondhand smoke during pregnancy are at an increased risk of delivering their babies prematurely, which can result in a higher likelihood of infant mortality. Additionally, it is noteworthy that even in cases where smokers' infants do not experience premature birth, they are commonly observed to exhibit obstructed respiratory passages and impaired pulmonary function at birth.

Secondary Exposure to Tobacco Smoke: An Overview

According to its formal definition, second-hand smoke pertains to the inhalation of environmental tobacco smoke by non-smokers, either involuntarily or passively.

Essential Facts Pertaining to the Hazards of Second-Hand Smoke

The inhalation of any quantity of tobacco smoke, be it directly or indirectly through second-hand exposure, poses detrimental effects to one's well-being. Exposure to passive smoking is associated with a multitude of significant health conditions. For example, the exposure to temporary secondhand smoke can heighten the likelihood of experiencing a cardiac arrest or trigger an immediate occurrence of a heart attack.

The Adverse Health Effects of Passive Smoking in the Adult Population

Secondhand smoke is responsible for an annual mortality rate of 600,000 among young individuals.

In addition, exposure to second-hand smoke leads to significant respiratory and cardiovascular disorders. This comprises ailments such as coronary heart disease and lung cancer. Secondary smoke exposure leads to untimely mortality in adult individuals. Additionally, it gives rise to the inhalation of highly toxic and carcinogenic chemicals by second-hand smokers. The aforementioned substances encompass formaldehyde, benzene, vinyl chloride, arsenic, ammonia, and hydrogen cyanide.

Adverse Health Effects in Children Resulting from Second-Hand Smoke Exposure

Secondhand smoking has a profoundly adverse impact on the health of children. It results in an estimated range of 150,000 to 300,000 infections in the lower respiratory tracts of children. It also causes an annual rate of 430 sudden infant death syndrome deaths. Additionally, exposure to second-hand smoke exacerbates respiratory symptoms in children with asthma, further compromising their health. Exposure to environmental tobacco smoke has been known to result in significantly reduced birth weights among infants born to individuals who smoke. In the year 2004, a significant 28% of child fatalities were directly attributed to the inhalation of second-hand smoke. However, it is important to note that roughly 40% of children are exposed to smoking due to having at least one smoking parent.

The Dangers of Smoking: Reasons to Cease Immediately!

1. Ceasing the habit of smoking is not as arduous as you perceive. Once you embark upon the path of genuine sincerity and objectively analyze the veracity surrounding the detrimental effects of smoking, you will find immense gratification in liberating yourself from this pernicious habit.

2. Confront the issue of your smoking habit. Please take it into consideration and assess it accordingly. Inquire explicitly about the specific benefits it is offering you, and subsequently reflect upon its limitations and areas where it may not meet your requirements. To commence, you can attend to your hair initially and gradually proceed to the extremities of your feet. Scientific evidence establishes that smoking exerts detrimental effects on every bodily organ, constituting a medical verity.

3. Consider reframing the act of quitting smoking as granting yourself a significant present. You are affording yourself an enhanced quality of life and, quite possibly, an extended lifespan. You are bestowing upon yourself a more robust physique. You are instilling a greater sense of self-assurance within

yourself. Furthermore, you are essentially allocating to yourself all the funds that are being frivolously expended on not only the purchase of cigarettes but also the resultant augmented costs associated with items such as health insurance and life insurance, albeit in the short term. Contemplate these circumstances as a valuable offering and do not hesitate to seize the opportunity."

4. Set a date. Make a dedication. Offer it a try. Please be aware that it is perfectly acceptable if you do not initially perform optimally. Merely keep trying. The solitary path to failure lies in ceasing one's efforts.

5. Do not regard it as an act of resignation. This gives the impression of

being excessive, akin to a loss. Essentially, you are discarding something from your life that has indeed caused harm and no longer has a place in your current circumstances. You are disposing of pure garbage. You are not going to permit your lungs to serve as a repository for nicotine and tar.

6. Maintain a positive mindset at all times. However, this is one of the most favorable actions you have ever undertaken. Avoid individuals with negative influence and steer clear of uncomfortable or tense circumstances.

7. Quit on your own. Although your family and loved ones will undoubtedly derive significant benefits from your decision to abstain, it is ultimately you who stands to gain the most advantages.

8. Approach the act of surrendering smoking with the appropriate level of respect it deserves. Ultimately become willing to go to great extents to eradicate it from your existence. In the event that you are unprepared, consider supplicating for the inclination. This often works.

9. Please consult your dictionary to research the term 'nicotine' and capture its definition prominently as follows: "A toxic alkaloid used as an agent for controlling pests." Place it in a visible location for easy reference.

10. Please refrain from asserting "I will take my chances" and continue to engage in smoking. They do not belong

to us for acquisition. We have not bestowed life upon ourselves, therefore it is not within our prerogative to gamble with the act of giving it away. That is within the realm of divine authority.

11. Do not deceive yourself by claiming to be burdened with numerous obligations that prevent you from quitting smoking. Engaging in smoking carries a substantial burden in itself. Each day carries a degree of uncertainty, as your very livelihood hangs in the balance. By eliminating nicotine from your lifestyle, you will find it easier to manage various other aspects of your life. You will experience significantly enhanced well-being and a notable increase in vitality. You will have succeeded in creating something far more meaningful than any amount of

wealth or material possessions you could ever amass. You will have bestowed upon yourself what no one else could conceivably bestow upon you. You shall be relieved from the burdens associated with tobacco consumption.

12. Please refrain from employing the justification of potential weight gain to rationalize your smoking habit. Furthermore, should you experience slight weight gain, it is imperative to acknowledge that your increased physical activity and exercise regimen will effectively counterbalance any such increase. It is important to bear in mind that weight gain is primarily caused by excessive food intake rather than the act of abstaining from smoking.

13. Formulate strategies to engage in activities that divert your attention from smoking. Occasionally, our thoughts can become formidable adversaries. They will inform us that we require a cigarette for virtually any circumstance that is convenient during that moment. By engaging in activities such as attending screenings in the smoke-free section, consuming popcorn or enjoying a lollipop, we can effectively occupy our minds and obtain a respite. Visit museums and other smoke-free establishments. Swimming is an excellent suggestion as well.

14. Refrain from smoking at each juncture and focus solely on the present moment. I shall refrain from smoking prior to midday." "I shall abstain from smoking until 3 o'clock." Occasionally, approach it incrementally by

considering each hour individually. This is significantly less complex in contrast to striving for everlasting cessation.

15. Don't subject on your own to smoky situations. In the event that you happen to come into contact with an individual who is smoking, it is appropriate to assert to yourself, "They are indulging in the act of smoking, while I am fortunate enough not to partake in such behavior."

16. While you are stopping. Kindly evaluate it as a potential investment. Once you have ceased your activities for a consecutive hour, you have dedicated this time towards improving your overall well-being. Now, allocate an additional hour for investment. Continue to incorporate in your investment on a regular basis. It will experience

continual growth and improvement as time progresses. The benefits of this investment will become increasingly apparent, not only in terms of tangible results but also in terms of personal satisfaction. Employ the same level of care and safeguarding as if it were a precious gem.

17. Commence exhibiting kindness towards yourself, as it signifies the commencement of a novel lifestyle for you, one in which you hold utmost significance. Sincerely value and honor yourself, while cultivating a deep sense of enthusiasm. Moreover, it is crucial to bear in mind that you are not continually introducing toxins into your body at frequent intervals. Inhale the pure atmosphere and do so with profound inhalation. Inhale the diverse and splendid aromas. Commence

frequenting outdoor areas in close proximity to notable features. There are a multitude of novel experiences that lie in store for you.

18. Do not get upset. When we experience anxiety or stress, our minds often suggest that smoking a cigarette is necessary for coping. Until one's consciousness acknowledges that cigarettes are not necessary for coping, it is advisable to steer clear of circumstances that may potentially predispose one to relapse. Refrain from associating with specific individuals who have the potential to cause you distress. If a significant level of stress is experienced in the workplace, it is advisable to consider taking a few days of leave. If it is not feasible for you to take an extended period of time off, consider refraining from smoking during

an extended holiday weekend. Exercise caution in regard to aspects such as acquiring embedded traffic, to the best of your ability. Exercise a high degree of caution. Anger has the potential for significant harm.

19. Do not get starving. It is remarkable how our cognitive faculties have the tendency to convince us that everything is amiss when merely satiating our hunger is the requisite action.

20. Please avoid excessive fatigue. Exhaustion often leads to irritability, and in such states of agitation, our minds tend to suggest that smoking a cigarette will provide relief. Our overall level of resistance is inherently weak, and it is relatively effortless to rationalize succumbing to the temptation and

saying, "Oh well, I suppose I shall engage in smoking."

21. Avoid feeling excessively isolated. It is beneficial to gain comprehension of individuals who are experiencing an identical situation. Attending Nicotine Anonymous conferences grants you the opportunity to acquire contact information of individuals facing similar challenges.

22. One should bear in mind the following four factors referred to as "HALT" which include hunger, anger, loneliness, and tiredness. If you have the inclination to smoke, please ascertain whether it is necessary. Ensure that none of these conditions are being experienced by you.

23. Do not exhaust yourself excessively. It proves challenging to abstain from smoking while remaining stationary. Keep hectic. Identify activities that bring you enjoyment. Engaging in cycling, indulging in hiking, partaking in swimming, exploring novel destinations, and embracing new culinary experiences. Now is the opportune moment to pamper yourself.

24. Acquire an object with which one can engage in repetitive manual movements. We have grown accustomed to holding a cigarette; the absence of one may leave our hands disoriented. Acquire a diminutive rubber sphere or a yo-yo. Play dough is equally favorable, or alternatively, a portion of clay.

25. Ensure you have something readily available to place in your oral cavity. Life Savers are enjoyable, or any variation of confectionery that slowly dissolves. Beef jerky and lollipops also provide assistance. Refrain from consuming high-calorie foods such as cookies. They have a relatively short duration of efficacy while also satiating your appetite. Conduct a research study whilst engaging in the act of smoking to determine which methods may alleviate the urge. If Life Savers are effective, then accumulate a reserve. Just a word of caution: refrain from utilizing this form of alternative for an extended duration.

26. If you consistently pair your coffee consumption with smoking, it is advised to discontinue coffee intake prior to initiating an effort to cease smoking.

27. Abstain from consuming alcoholic beverages during your period of cessation. Once alcohol enters your system, your physiological defenses will undergo a significant reduction.

28. Please be advised that the discomfort you may encounter during the initial two-week period will ultimately subside, and you will not have to endure it again in the future.

29. Regularly give on your own a congrats. What you are doing isn't easy whatsoever. Attempting to quit smoking requires substantial courage.

30. If you are experiencing discomfort as a result of withdrawal symptoms, allow it to serve as a enduring recollection to serve as a reminder of the formidable nature of the drug nicotine and the extent of your addiction.

31. Please consider that cigarettes were depleting your vitality. Please refrain from granting them any additional permissions.

32. Prevent the self-pity trap. If we begin to indulge in self-pity, our thoughts may persuade us to resort to smoking as a means to genuinely uplift our spirits.

33. Please be aware that persevering in your endeavors will ultimately lead to

success. It surpasses adversity and moreover the circumstances are favorable to you.

34. Prior to relinquishing, strategize your pursuits for the initial period following your resignation. By following this approach, you will be relieved of the burden of making numerous decisions during the withdrawal process. At first, making a decision can be challenging in the absence of a cigarette.

35. If you do not intend to resign promptly, then commence the process of reducing your workload. If you engage in the consumption of two packs of cigarettes daily and gradually reduce your intake by one cigarette each day over the course of a month, your daily consumption will ultimately reduce to a

mere total of 10 cigarettes per day. Nevertheless, certain individuals have found the act of decreasing their intake to be nearly as challenging as abstaining altogether.

36. Consume ample amounts of fluids to facilitate the elimination of toxins from your body. Orange juice is a beneficial choice given that smoking diminishes the level of vitamin C in our bodies.

37. Keep in mind, it is the initial cigarette that initiates the process. It takes just one. This is the item that you currently lack. You may choose to defer the act of igniting the initial one for a short duration. Do not engage in self-deception and believe that you can commence and cease at your own discretion. You cannot. Numerous

individuals have made attempts and subsequently found themselves unable to attain liberation from the grip of nicotine for the remainder of their lives.

38. Frequently make a conscious effort to reflect upon the observations you have made about yourself. Points like: Your breath not smells like a dirty ashtray. Your teeth are exhibiting a visible reduction in their yellow tint, while also appearing noticeably vibrant and impeccably cleansed. Your fingers remain free from tarnish caused by tobacco usage. The chronic coughing exhibited by the individual who appears unhealthy due to smoking is steadily diminishing. Your olfactory and gustatory senses are being restored. There has been a notable improvement in the condition of your skin. Your overall attitude towards oneself has

greatly improved, as you are increasingly demonstrating genuine self-care.

39. Offer it away. Whenever you find a chance to extend your expertise, support, and intention to another individual who smokes, seize it. This act of generosity will not only assist you in abstaining from nicotine but also provide support for your endeavor. Assisting individuals in breaking free from this detrimental substance yields significant benefits.

40. Have a follow-up program. Do not assume beyond the granted fact that you have successfully persevered for a few weeks. Nicotine is really shrewd. Please persist in attending Nicotine Anonymous conferences. In the event that there are

no scheduled meetings in your locality, support will be provided to facilitate the establishment of a new one. It is very easy. You only require a suitable venue and a few individuals who are interested.

41. When desiring to engage in smoking, please peruse this comprehensive compilation of recommendations.

Your Progression Of Abstinence: First, Second, And Third Days

Thus, the date of your departure has now arrived. Congratulations! Prior to commencing, kindly allocate a moment to inhale deeply and assess the state of your emotions. You might have an urge for a cigarette. Indeed, I would be thoroughly astonished if you were not. Nevertheless, endeavor to transcend that and ascertain precisely the state of your emotions. Are you apprehensive? Excited? A little sad even? Rest assured, the range of emotions you are experiencing is entirely normal. It is probable that you will experience a range of emotions during the forthcoming two weeks. Rest assured, I shall guide you patiently and meticulously throughout this cessation process, spanning a duration of two weeks. You will acquire strategies to effectively manage cravings for cigarettes without experiencing weight gain, while also mitigating potential side effects associated with smoking cessation. If you are prepared, we can now commence with your initial 24-hour period.

Embarking Upon Your Inaugural Day as a Non-smoker

Congratulations on embarking on the initial stage towards liberating yourself from the grasp of smoking. The primary point to consider is that you will experience cravings. There will manifest intense cravings to engage in smoking, which give the perception that your entire being is yearning for nicotine. Nonetheless, it is important to consider two factors. Initially, the duration of cravings generally does not exceed a span of two or three minutes. If you can abstain from the act of reaching for your cigarettes during this duration, you will successfully overcome the ensuing desire.

Do you recall our previous conversation in which I advised against discarding your cigarettes, lighter, and ashtray? There exists a compelling rationale for this. Should you choose to eliminate all cigarettes and smoking paraphernalia from your residence, you may perceive the cessation of smoking as compelled rather than self-determined. It is of great significance that each instance of overcoming a craving is a result of one's voluntary determination, rather than being compelled to do so. Please gather all of your smoking paraphernalia and securely seal it within a drawer.

Now, it is essential to ensure that you maintain a healthy diet. It is crucial to consume a nutritious breakfast upon awakening because the act of ceasing to smoke will lead to a decrease in your blood sugar levels. Irrespective of whether you typically forgo breakfast, it is imperative that you partake in the morning meal, particularly within the initial three days. It is advisable to consume significant quantities of pure, unadulterated fruit juices. It is advisable to refrain from consuming foods high in fat or sugar, as these can exacerbate the adverse effects associated with smoking.

Please bear in mind that there will be triggers that it would be wise to steer clear of. Therefore, it is important to make a firm commitment to abstain from consuming alcohol over the course of the forthcoming fortnight, and to acquire a suitable alternative to nicotine for times when these triggers arise. Several exemplary alternatives include sugar-free hard candies, cinnamon sticks or flavored toothpicks, and sunflower seeds.

Following the consumption of breakfast, there exist specific actions one can undertake to enhance one's morale and divert one's attention from smoking. Presented below is a compilation of endeavors designed to enhance one's self-esteem and cultivate sustained motivation towards maintaining a healthy lifestyle, free from smoking. Please experiment with a few of these options, or feel free to try all of them, should you wish to do so. We encourage you to return tomorrow to continue with Day Two.

Engage in a leisurely stroll, particularly with a specific objective in mind, such as visiting an acquaintance who does not partake in smoking.

Engage in additional vigorous physical activities such as tennis or another dynamic pursuit that can distract your thoughts from smoking.

Select one room in your residence and thoroughly clean it, ensuring all areas are cleansed meticulously. If you possess an entire day uninterrupted, you can undertake the task of cleaning the entire household. It is remarkable how greatly one's inclination to quit smoking can be influenced by the presence of a clean and immaculate living environment.

Engage in outdoor chores such as tending to the yard, cultivating a garden, or carrying out landscaping activities.

Engage in a creative endeavor that you have been desiring to undertake. Ensure that it sufficiently occupies your mind to divert any thoughts related to cigarettes.

Second Day: You Display Remarkable Ability!

If you have reached this stage in the book, having successfully abstained from smoking for a continuous period of 24 hours, my warmest congratulations are due to you. If successfully abstaining from tobacco consumption were akin to the esteemed Marine Corps, you would undoubtedly be on a commendable trajectory towards eligibility for the renowned SEALS division. You belong to the privileged class. However, we have a full day's worth of time remaining.

The second day is anticipated to be more challenging in contrast to the initial day. Do not be caught off guard by sudden, unforeseen desires. Remain composed and remind yourself that you have successfully completed one-third of Phase One, and you will not jeopardize your progress by resuming smoking. Should your mind deceive you into believing that a solitary cigarette has no adverse effects, it speaks erroneously. The progression from smoking a single cigarette to another, followed by subsequent cigarettes, will ultimately result in a return to regular smoking habits.

Utilize this day as an opportunity to set personal objectives. You have the option to utilize the computer, or alternatively, employ poster board and magic markers. However, it is crucial to ensure that you are engaged in productive activities, accessing your non-nicotine replacement product upon experiencing cues, and directing your focus towards personal development. If you find yourself with surplus time after establishing personal objectives, dedicating time to exercise is advisable. Additionally, it is opportune to conclude the cleaning of your residence. Engaging in physical activity will induce the release of substances within the body that can emulate the sensations typically associated with tobacco use. Under no circumstances should you approach that drawer. You have nearly overcome the most challenging phase.

The primary objective of Day Two is to locate a sauna facility and spend a significant amount of time in relaxation within its confines. To mitigate the potential adverse reactions of ceasing nicotine consumption and prevent weight loss, it is desirable to expel nicotine from one's system expeditiously. Participating in a session of sauna bathing will facilitate the elimination of a significant amount of nicotine through perspiration.

Day Three: You Have Emerged Victorious!

Accordingly, we have now entered the initial stages of the third day. If you have adhered to my guidelines regarding the usage of a sauna, your experience on Day Three will likely be significantly more manageable compared to the majority of individuals. You may encounter certain cravings, however, the sauna session should have provided a significant uplift on Day Three.

Devote the day to being absent from one's place of residence. Engage in recreational activities such as casually browsing retail displays, or partake in cultural pursuits by visiting a museum, art gallery, or attending a theatrical performance. Make every effort to expedite the passage of time throughout the day. Should you encounter any adverse effects resulting from smoking, rest assured that they will be transient, attributable to the synergistic effects of rejuvenation achieved through sauna therapy and engagement in enjoyable pastimes.

Ultimately, recline and commend yourself. You have successfully confronted and conquered one of the most arduous challenges you have encountered, and there is no retracing your steps at this point. You have successfully abstained from smoking for a duration of 72 hours, and now you can find solace in the knowledge that the remainder of your journey will be relatively effortless. In the upcoming Chapter Six, we will delve into strategies ensuring adherence to your tobacco-free journey, maintaining your progress over the course of the following 12 days until achieving a full two weeks of abstinence.

Timetable And Regimen

The Significance of Timetable Management

Creating a well-structured timetable for your days and weeks, establishing a consistent routine that fosters optimal vitality, will serve as a fundamental prerequisite when endeavoring to bring about a transformation. Don't overlook the importance of putting pen to paper, writing a schedule and routine. I must admit, my adherence to traditional practices has caused me to overlook the fact that we now have access to scheduling applications that can be conveniently installed on our mobile devices in this contemporary era.

Establishing and adhering to a structured timetable and regimen, striving to maintain a high level of adherence, is of significant importance. The timing and approach you choose will assist you in establishing a foundation for your daily activities. Establish a consistent schedule for your daily activities, enabling you to identify the stimuli you will encounter during your regular regimen.

The effective organization of your daily activities can significantly impact the outcome of your cessation efforts.

Establishing a prevailing trend will impact your psychological well-being and furnish a cadence to assimilate as you progress.

Biorhythms

The fluctuations in your biorhythms over the course of the day impact your emotional, physical, and cognitive functioning. Take careful notice of the moments in your day that will exert the greatest influence on your overall well-being. By assessing oneself, documenting one's emotions and performance at different intervals throughout the day, an individual can gain sufficient self-awareness to establish a secure and well-organized routine.

Maintain a well-structured schedule and consistent routine in order to remain within a state of comfort. Establish specific schedules for all activities to ensure efficient time management. If necessary, consider setting alarms for all your activities in order to establish a consistent rhythm. You may wish to employ the calendar function on your mobile device for this purpose. There are certainly alternative applications that you may use; nevertheless, it is advisable to employ any tool that will assist you in remaining organized and focused.

I would suggest devising a meticulously planned schedule prior to commencing the week, and endeavoring to adhere to it. Prior to resigning, it is advisable to diligently engage in this activity for a period of a few weeks while consistently conducting thorough evaluations on a daily basis, thereby facilitating the identification of areas that warrant adjustment throughout the course of each week. Prepare for potential obstacles that have the potential to disrupt your normal routine. Anticipate this situation, yet maintain a mindset that allows you to return to your original agenda. In the event of veering off course, promptly revert to your predetermined strategy.

Please ensure to incorporate that element of self-care into your weekly routine. It is advisable to refrain from enduring each week without dedicating time for personal well-being. Engage in activities such as bathing, watching television, authoring a book, playing a musical instrument, or partaking in a period of rest. Make an effort to engage in activities that promote relaxation or enjoyment throughout the course of your week. You'll need it.

Summary

In conclusion, devise a timetable that is suitable for your needs. Develop or procure a digital or physical agenda tool that is most suitable for your needs in order to establish and uphold a consistent schedule for all days of the week. Plan for possible hiccups. Make an effort to promptly regain your rhythm if you veer off course. Please ensure to allocate time for self-care in order to ensure your well-being and personal enjoyment throughout the week.

The Challenges Of Smoking Cessation: Understanding The Difficulty

Perhaps you have made attempts to cease this habit before, and perchance you have also encountered individuals who have ventured down the same path, only to find themselves unable to achieve success. Why is it so hard to stop smoking? Nicotine, the addictive substance present in cigarettes, bears full responsibility for all the culpability in this matter.

Nicotine: The Culprit

What is it about the chemical composition of nicotine that creates a formidable challenge when attempting to overcome its grip? Nicotine is a compound, commonly referred to as a psychoactive substance, present in tobacco. It induces a temporary euphoric sensation, akin to the effects induced by highly addictive narcotics such as cocaine and heroin. Nicotine has the capacity to influence individuals through two distinct yet interconnected mechanisms: physical addiction and psychological reliance, forming a steadfast alliance that hinders efforts to cease smoking.

When engaging in smoking, the nicotine present in tobacco is transported to the pulmonary organs and subsequently circulated within your cardiovascular system. This harmful substance is disseminated throughout the entirety of the human body, ultimately reaching the brain at an accelerated rate surpassing that of any intravenous drug consumption. Considering its distribution throughout the entirety of one's physique, it exerts an impact on the entire physiological framework, particularly on vascular structures, pulmonary function, cerebral activity, and metabolic processes. It may also be transferred via the mammary glands and detected in the breast milk of pregnant individuals who smoke. Furthermore, it has the ability to traverse the placental barrier, ultimately manifesting in the amniotic fluid and umbilical cord of the developing fetus.

The onset of nicotine dependence occurs once the toxic compound infiltrates the brain through the act of smoking. It elicits delightful sensations and induces a transitory euphoria. This positive sensation would elicit a desire to resume smoking. Paradoxically, nicotine can also function as a depressant due to its ability to disrupt the transmission of signals within the nervous system. This can potentially induce feelings of anxiety and elicit a desire to resume smoking. An individual may persuade themselves to smoke just one more cigarette, always with the intention of keeping the promise, yet nicotine's influence often leads to the breaking of such promises. The augmentation of this behavioral cycle amplifies the nicotine levels in the bloodstream.

With the progression of smoking, individuals build up a tolerance to nicotine. Consequently, it implies that an elevated dosage of nicotine is indispensably needed in order to elicit a commensurate response as compared to the initial stages of tobacco consumption. Over time, there is a gradual rise in tolerance levels, thereby resulting in escalated smoking habits.

Once a specific quantity of cigarettes has been consumed, the nicotine concentration declines, resulting in the cessation of the pleasurable sensation. Upon experiencing this, one may encounter feelings of irritability or discomfort. With the ignition of yet another stick, the pleasurable sensations resurface, initiating a perpetuation of this ongoing pattern.

Physical Addiction: Withdrawal Symptoms

The cessation of substance use induces withdrawal symptoms due to the presence of physical dependency. These symptoms are commonly associated with a high degree of discomfort. These are the physiological and neurological responses exhibited by the human body and brain when nicotine is not present. Individuals who engage in smoking on a regular basis may experience withdrawal symptoms upon abruptly discontinuing or significantly reducing their tobacco consumption. The symptoms typically commence subsequent to the consumption of the final cigarette and intensify within a 2-3 day period, during which the residual nicotine by-products remain present within the body. The duration of the symptoms may extend from days to weeks; however, sustained abstinence from smoking promotes improvement in the smoker's condition.

Withdrawal symptoms include:

Dizziness and headaches

Intense cigarette cravings

Sweating

Depression, anxiety, irritability

Insomnia

Difficulty in staying focused

Restlessness and fatigue

Enhance appetite and promote weight gain

Properly and accurately managing these symptoms will enhance the likelihood of successfully achieving smoking cessation.

Psychological Dependency: Struggling to Overcome Patterns

In addition to the physical dependency on nicotine, the emotional and cognitive well-being is also impacted. Smoking has been regarded as a mechanism for alleviating stress, anxiety, and even ennui for certain individuals. Should you choose to cease, an additional catalyst for the resumption of smoking would arise when you encounter adverse emotions. The enjoyable sensation that arises from the presence of nicotine within one's body is yearned for. On an emotional level, this experience can be likened to parting ways with a close confidant, and on a cognitive level, it signifies a significant shift in one's behavioral patterns.

In addition, it is customary for individuals who smoke to integrate this habit into their daily rituals and routines. Smoking can often become a reflexive action concomitant to one's morning coffee, pre or post meals, during work breaks, or while socializing with acquaintances or loved ones. In order to successfully initiate cessation, it is imperative to acquire knowledge regarding both the addictive nature and accompanying behavioral patterns associated with smoking.

Your environment and you.

During a recent book promotional tour in China, I had the opportunity to visit the captivating city of Guangdong, where I resided for a few days. In the early hours of the morning, I made the decision to embark on a leisurely walk. As I was preparing to depart from the hotel where I had been lodged, a member of the hotel staff hastily approached me and handed me a sanitary mask-like item. It is essential to have this item with you should you venture outdoors. Her speech was characterized by a prominent, twangy Chinese accent. With a sense of puzzlement, I accepted the provided mask and began my departure. Upon passing through the polished double doors, a transformed environment presented itself before me, starkly contrasting the splendid cityscape I had observed mere days before - a sight that justified her insistence on donning a protective face covering. The entire area was immersed in a dense haze of smog. The atmosphere was imbued with an unsettling quality, reminiscent of a dense fog that instinctively compelled one to blink more frequently. The sensation was nearly palpable. The level of visibility was mildly impacted, as vehicles were proceeding at a speed of mere 30 kilometers per hour with their headlights illuminated during the morning traffic. That clearly marked my initial encounter and firsthand exposure to the smog prevalent in Chinese urban areas. Nevertheless, the most captivating spectacle that commanded my focus was the scene I encountered at an intersection, situated a short distance from my location. A cluster of youthful males meandered, casually inhaling on cigarettes, amidst the hazy shroud enveloping their surroundings.

Smoking in smog? What is delaying you, if I may inquire? Despite the proximity at which those powerful trucks pass by? One could equally consider placing oneself beneath the substantial wheels, as the subsequent outcome to be endured following the inhalation of copious amounts of noxious smog combined with tobacco is significantly more intricate, distressing, and exorbitantly costly than one may perceive.

For individuals residing in urban areas with consistently low air quality and engaging in heavy smoking, it is not a matter of complexity to comprehend that one's life expectancy will diminish to less than a quarter of their current age.

Why engage in smoking while residing in an environment with elevated risks? Why accelerate your demise or contribute to your detriment when you have the opportunity to mitigate the hazards and protect your well-being by altering your noxious surroundings? Relocate. Trade your comfort for a state of wellness. Living or perishing in an unfavorable setting undoubtedly hampers one's comfort and well-being. However, the likelihood of recuperation and a prolonged lifespan is assured if one chooses to reside or relocate to a more healthful environment characterized by cleaner air.

We have now reached the last stage...

Creating A Quit Plan

Thorough preparation is imperative for achieving success. In order to effectively cease the habit of smoking and maintain a smoke-free lifestyle, it is imperative to adequately equip oneself for any eventualities. You are required to possess knowledge regarding the necessary procedures to be undertaken, as well as an understanding of potential obstacles that may arise. In this manner, you can devise strategies to effectively address or surmount these challenges.

How to Develop an Effective Cessation Strategy

Developing a cessation strategy serves as an optimal approach to ready oneself for the cessation of smoking. It has the potential to enhance the likelihood of your success and equip you with the ability to effectively confront the obstacles that arise during the process of cessation. It is possible to employ a variety of strategies in order to maintain confidence, motivation, and focus.

The subsequent instructions outline the requisite measures for formulating a cessation strategy. If you find yourself unsure of where to begin, it would be prudent to adhere to their established course. Please consider these as references to assist you in formulating your own. As you progress through these stages, ensure to maintain a comprehensive documentation of your cessation strategy. By following this approach, you will be able to monitor your progress and guarantee your achievement.

Select a quit date.

It is advised that you select an earliest possible date of cessation. Many smokers choose a date within a couple of weeks. This affords them ample time to make necessary preparations. It is advisable to refrain from choosing a month or week that is highly occupied. Please mark your intended cessation date on your calendar for immediate visibility. Please ensure that you store the information on your mobile device to facilitate the receipt of timely notifications.

Request the assistance of immediate family members and close acquaintances.

Inform your loved ones about your decision to quit and ask them to help you in this endeavor. Inform them about the intended date of cessation so that they could extend their support and aid. Request their assistance, such as enlisting their support in discouraging your proximity to cigarettes, declining your participation in smoking, and accompanying you to venues where you can enjoy yourself without engaging in smoking activities.

Assistance is crucial for achieving success. With the presence of a supportive network comprised of family, friends, and colleagues, feelings of isolation are alleviated, rendering the process of quitting significantly more manageable. "If you encounter challenges in seeking assistance, here are some guidelines to adhere to:

Please provide explicit details regarding your desires and/or requirements.

It is unrealistic to anticipate that others will possess the ability to perceive your thoughts without any verbal or non-verbal cues from you. Consequently, it is imperative that you communicate your desires and/or requirements to them. Kindly communicate your specific expectations regarding the assistance you require in order to facilitate the process of quitting. As an illustration, in the event that you find yourself burdened with stress following an arduous day and seek solace in the consumption of a cigarette, you may politely request the assistance of a trusted acquaintance or co-worker in facilitating diversionary activities. You have the option to visit a coffee shop or dine at a restaurant that prohibits smoking. Ensure that you request their assistance with courtesy and politeness. These individuals are endeavoring to assist you. Therefore, it is imperative that you express appreciation for their endeavors.

Avoid stressful situations.

Stress has the ability to induce smoking behavior. Therefore, it is advisable to minimize exposure to situations that induce stress. Recall your stressors. Please ascertain the factors, individuals, or objects that commonly evoke feelings of stress for you. Please notify your family and friends about these stressors in order to enlist their assistance in avoiding them.

Say 'thank you'.

Inform your family members, acquaintances, and professional associates that you acknowledge and value the efforts they have put forth. Inform them directly, transmit written correspondence such as text messages and e-mails, or make an effort to contact them by phone to extend gratitude. Additionally, you have the option of bestowing gifts upon them or inviting them to dine out as a means of expressing gratitude and making them feel valued.

Associate yourself with individuals whom you genuinely admire and have confidence in.

Choose to associate exclusively with individuals who positively contribute to your self-perception. Sever connections with acquaintances and even blood relatives who contribute to your emotional distress. Please be reminded that the duration of your acquaintance holds no significance. If the dynamics of your friendship or relationship have ceased to serve your best interests, it is imperative that you relinquish it. Breaking connections with them may present challenges, but it is imperative for the preservation of your personal welfare. Direct your attention to individuals who provide support and genuinely desire to witness your successful transformation.

Invest in personal relationships.

Refrain from dedicating excessive amounts of time to work or operating a business. While the significance of your career and professional networks cannot be understated, it is equally imperative to duly cherish and nurture your personal relationships. Reach out to acquaintances and relatives with whom you have been out of touch for a significant duration. Merely engaging in communication with them can significantly enhance your emotional well-being and engender a sense of improved mood.

Support other people.

Support, in reality, encompasses mutual exchange. If one desires to receive support from others, it is imperative to reciprocate and offer support to others as well. Assist your family, acquaintances, and associates however you are able. Give them moral support. Elevate their spirits through the sharing of humorous anecdotes or jokes. Smile at them. Providing assistance to individuals in times of need can facilitate the establishment of stronger interpersonal bonds.

Remove all smoking stimuli.

Common smoking cues often encompass cigarettes, lighters, matches, and ashtrays. Having these items present within your household can contribute to an increased propensity for tobacco consumption. Please dispose of them or place them in storage. Alternatively, you may also request others to ensure the absence of these items during your visits to their residences.

Maintain cleanliness in your residence, automobile, and place of work.

For the majority of individuals, the mere scent of smoke is sufficient to compel them to ignite a cigarette. This is the rationale for ensuring the maintenance of a clean and refreshing environment. Maintaining a well-ordered living and professional environment can enhance one's productivity as well. Therefore, you can redirect your attention towards more significant matters and alleviate the habit of smoking.

Reiterate your motives and exercise caution regarding potential triggers.

Given that you have already established your rationales for resigning and identified your triggers, ensure that you consistently reinforce them to yourself. In this manner, you will maintain your motivation in the pursuit of your objective to become smoke-free. It is recommended to diligently record them and prominently display duplicate copies of your inventory in easily accessible locations. It is also advisable to maintain electronic copies of your list on both your smartphone and computer.

Similarly, it is important for you to be cognizant of your triggers. When you are aware of the likelihood of encountering a trigger, exert effort to steer clear of it. As an illustration, should your commuting path encompass a tobacco establishment, it would be advisable to opt for an alternate route. If you receive an invitation to attend a gathering in which individuals are anticipated to engage in smoking and consuming alcoholic beverages, it is recommended that you politely decline.

Develop strategies for coping.

Once you cease the habit of smoking, your physiological framework adapts to the absence of nicotine. Your physique undergoes the phase of withdrawal, which can be disagreeable yet not insurmountable. It is imperative that you employ effective coping mechanisms to alleviate your symptoms and facilitate seamless integration into society.

One possible way to rephrase this sentence in a formal tone could be: "By implementing modifications in behavior and incorporating pharmaceutical interventions, one can effectively mitigate symptoms." There exists a multitude of medications that can be obtained without the need for a prescription. Please ensure that you have them available in your inventory prior to closing. In this manner, you can promptly address your symptoms as soon as they manifest. As each day of therapy progresses, your symptoms gradually diminish.

Chapter 2

Methods

Now that you have discerned the underlying cause of your smoking habit, it is imperative to determine an effective strategy to cease this behavior. Similar to all addictions, the underlying causes are highly individualistic. Consequently, the approach towards cessation will vary significantly for each individual. Peruse the various approaches and discern which ones you are inclined to experiment with. In the event that the first approach proves unsuccessful, it is advisable to attempt an alternative method. However, identify a single option and commit to it, ensuring that you follow through until the end. It is essential for you to discern, by thoroughly perusing the methodologies, the one that aligns with your own sensibilities. Choose the alternative that you are confident will yield favorable results. A significant number of individuals tend to unconsciously opt for a task that they possess a high probability of failing. They engage in this activity with the intention of subsequently shrugging and expressing, "I made an attempt, but cessation proved exceedingly challenging." They commence with an initial inclination towards failure. Alter your mindset promptly, and commence with a proactive attitude geared towards achieving success. That is undoubtedly the most reliable method to achieve success. So let's get started!

Doctor

A significant number of individuals experience a greater sense of ease when engaging in conversations with their healthcare provider in comparison to confiding in a therapist. Fortunately, your physician possesses comprehensive knowledge regarding the detrimental impact of smoking on your physical well-being. Moreover, they can perform tests that specifically exhibit the progressive deterioration of your body caused by this habit. Subsequently, the physician may propose a variety of pharmaceutical options that you may wish to contemplate.

Chantix is a pharmaceutical solution specifically designed to assist individuals seeking to quit smoking through prescription-based intervention. (also known as Varenicline)

Bupropion plays a vital role in mitigating the symptoms of nicotine withdrawal. (also known as Zyban)

Pharmacological intervention for nicotine addiction

Similar to any pharmaceutical treatment, there exists the potential for both dependency and adverse reactions. Hence, it is of utmost importance to communicate in a transparent and honest manner with your physician prior to making any decisions regarding the consumption of these substances. Your physician possesses superior knowledge regarding which substances you ought to consume or avoid.

Go cold turkey

The precise denotation of 'cold turkey' is the sudden and total termination of drug consumption by an individual grappling with addiction. This approach has been successful for numerous individuals and, despite its significant efficacy, it is undeniably one of the most challenging methods. It necessitates a considerable amount of resilience, eagerness, and resolve.

Establish a specified date: the presence of a definitive quitting date holds significant importance. If you persist in uttering the phrase 'someday I shall resign,' you shall never actually do so. Whether you choose to take action today or establish a specific date at which you intend to cease, the decision remains yours. After acquiring the date, proceed to document it and affix it in a visible location. Please be aware that, following the specified date, you will be actively choosing to embark on a transformative journey towards enhancing your life. Ensure that the date is communicated to all individuals involved, in order to establish their accountability for its execution.

Acquire knowledge of the potential adverse effects: notwithstanding that abruptly quitting without assistance constitutes the optimal approach for enhancing your overall well-being, it also entails enduring withdrawal symptoms. Having knowledge of this fact and comprehending that it merely presents an obstacle that must be surmounted, will aid in facilitating the procedure. Certain adverse reactions may manifest, namely irritability, anxiety, excessive perspiration, sleep disturbances, depressive symptoms, and difficulty concentrating. These symptoms may manifest with considerable severity, coupled with a strong inclination to relapse into smoking.

Develop a comprehensive strategy: it is insufficient to simply make the decision to quit and assume that will bring resolution to the matter. Certainly, the process is both laborious and challenging, necessitating a strategic approach to successfully navigate through it. Keep a journal. Phone a friend. Ensure the presence of a family member. Take up a hobby. Exercise. Eat well. Discover nutritious snacks to suppress the desire. Conduct thorough research and engage in extensive reading on the subject of cessation. The greater your reading habits, the broader your knowledge base will become, consequently enhancing your ability to overcome challenges. Certain individuals discover methods of relaxation through the practice of meditation, while others find solace in engaging in vigorous physical activity. It is imperative that you identify the technique that best suits your personal needs and preferences.

Exercise self-restraint: possessing cigarettes within your residence increases the likelihood of succumbing to the temptation of smoking one. The consumption of even a single unit will invariably lead to the consumption of the entire set, perpetuating the relentless pattern. Ensure that your household, workplace, and vehicle are devoid of any temptations. One will not desire what they lack.

Please be aware that it typically takes approximately two to three weeks for the withdrawal symptoms to subside. Subsequently, any residual appetites you may experience will stem from psychological rather than physical factors. Following a few weeks of abstinence, you will eliminate any physiological reliance on nicotine.

A craving Journal

Many individuals find writing to be highly therapeutic, and it is commonly advised across various forms of addiction as a means of promoting healing. Employing a journal in tandem with alternative modalities would be highly advantageous and present a commendable avenue for discerning the timing, catalysts, social context, location, and actionable measures to instigate a transformation in smoking behavior. Having it documented in written form is a commendable approach to identifying areas where errors may occur. It also serves as an effective method for monitoring and gauging one's progress throughout the journey. Maintaining a personal journal can be highly beneficial; however, it can be even more advantageous to utilize a diary in the form of a blog. In this manner, you are able to disseminate your experiences to a broader audience. Exhort others to accompany you on your pursuit, thereby cultivating a collective of individuals who are traversing similar challenges. This offers a valuable opportunity to connect with individuals who share similar interests and mutually motivate one another along this path.

Nicotine Replacement Therapy

Nicotine Replacement Therapy, also referred to as NRT, entails various methods for substituting nicotine. The issue associated with NRT stems from the fact that a considerable number of individuals subsequently develop a dependence on these alternative methods. It is imperative that you diligently adhere to the instructions provided and establish specific dates for gradually discontinuing its usage. For certain individuals, these methods prove efficacious, while for others, they do not serve as a viable solution. Please exercise caution and consider pursuing this option only if it is necessary. If you find yourself getting addicted then stop.

Patches: The transdermal application of nicotine patches facilitates the controlled release of nicotine into the bloodstream. Subsequently, you gradually reduce your dependence by gradually acquainting yourself with patches of lower dosage. This has proven to be beneficial to a significant number of individuals, particularly when faced with early morning cravings.

Nicotine gum is readily available for purchase without a prescription, and is offered in 2mg and 4mg potencies. The choice between gum and patch is entirely at your discretion; nonetheless, one advantageous aspect of gum utilization is the ability to regulate the desired quantity, although it is important to note that some individuals may perceive this as a disadvantage. It is recommended to take a maximum of two doses per hour as per the prescribed schedule.

To procure nicotine nasal spray, one must first obtain a prescription from a physician. It exhibits rapid efficacy due to its immediate absorption into the bloodstream via the nasal route. It is advised to refrain from using the spray for a duration exceeding six months, as adverse effects may manifest over time, including excessive tear production, bouts of sneezing, and irritation of the throat and nasal passages. It is contraindicated for individuals with nasal conditions, highlighting the utmost importance of consulting with a medical professional beforehand.

A doctor's prescription is required prior to utilizing the nicotine inhaler as a method of therapy. It yields a comparable sensation to tobacco consumption, with the prescribed quantity ranging from 4 to 20 cartridges per day, necessitating a gradual reduction over approximately six months.

Lozenges: These are readily available for purchase without a prescription, offering options in 2mg and 4mg potencies. This is contingent upon the frequency of your previous tobacco consumption, therefore it is advisable to exercise moderation unless it is deemed necessary. The prescribed procedure for consuming a lozenge entails gradually letting it dissolve inside the mouth until complete dissolution occurs, typically lasting approximately twenty to thirty minutes. It is imperative to refrain from chewing or swallowing the substance, instead allowing for sufficient time for absorption through the oral cavity.

Therapist

Engaging the services of a counselor to assist you in navigating the process of quitting holds great merit, as it enables you to benefit from the expertise and experience of a seasoned professional. The therapist will have the capacity to customize a plan that caters to your needs, which is exceedingly advantageous. It presents an excellent forum for individuals to express their grievances and articulate their concerns without reservation. A therapist could potentially assist you in gaining insight into the underlying factors contributing to your smoking behavior.

Hypnosis

Hypnosis is a state of consciousness characterized by a modified state of sleep while maintaining complete awareness. According to popular belief, being in this state purportedly enables individuals to delve into the depths of their subconscious mind, which would otherwise be inaccessible in a normal state. Numerous individuals held the belief that this modified state denotes the pinnacle of relaxation, rendering one particularly receptive to suggestions.

Herbert Spiegel was a renowned American psychiatrist who significantly contributed to the popularization of hypnosis as a medical intervention. His methodologies revolved around three primary concepts: 1. Smoking is detrimental to the body. The human body is crucial for sustaining life, indicating a necessity for its existence. It is imperative to exhibit reverence for one's physical well-being and ensure its preservation.

The patient was instructed in the practice of self-hypnosis, wherein they would employ these affirmations as a coping mechanism whenever an inclination to smoke arose.

There exists a plethora of alternative hypnosis techniques to explore, with a significant number of practitioners who continue to engage in this discipline in the present day.

Support Groups

There exists an abundant array of support groups worldwide, along with an extensive online community encompassing individuals who facilitate groups and programs. Participating actively constitutes an excellent approach towards aiding your endeavor to cease, owing to the substantial networks of support and easily accessible wealth of information. Participating in digital discourse and engaging in virtual forums can provide significant therapeutic benefits, along with serving as an invaluable platform for acquiring answers to queries of any nature. The actions of individuals in our vicinity have a profound impact on us as human beings, making it imperative to selectively associate ourselves with individuals who exude positivity.

A Concise Chronological Account Of The Origins And Evolution Of Hypnosis

Hypnosis has been in existence since ancient times. I have consistently been intrigued by the following verse excerpted from the sacred text, the Bible:

Genesis 2:21 "The Lord God induced a profound slumber upon the man, and he entered a state of sleep: thereafter, He extracted one of his ribs and diligently sealed the void with flesh."

Can it be inferred from the text of Genesis, the initial book of the Old Testament within the Bible, that the

Lord God had employed hypnosis to carry out a surgical procedure on Adam?

During the era predating recorded history, it is plausible that hypnosis served as the sole modality for the purposes of healing or pain management. Trance has been employed by all early civilizations as a means of facilitating the process of healing.

In the year 1998, I had the privilege of undertaking an extended period of time in the presence of the Kuna Indians. The Kuna people inhabit a stretch of approximately 150 miles encompassing both dense forests and islands, which is known as the San Blas Archipelago, located off the Caribbean coastline of Panama.

The Kuna are among the few remaining indigenous populations of the Caribbean region. They engage in hunting, fishing, coconut cultivation, and small-scale agriculture within the confines of jungle clearings. They continue to reside in dwellings characterized by thatched roofs and engage in the practice of cooking using open fires.

Each Kuna village is governed by the Saila (Chief) and the Nele (Shaman), who uphold impeccable concordance within their community through a sophisticated framework of regulations.

The ailing individuals are brought before the Nele (Shaman), who employs melodious incantations to induce a state of trance. I had the privilege of observing the process of healing and was awestruck when the patient under the guidance of the shaman entered a state resembling a hypnotic trance.

On a different occasion, I found myself situated in a distant Mayan settlement situated on the shores of Lake Atitlan in the elevated regions of Guatemala. I have discovered the location where the effigy of the deity, Machimon, was stored throughout the entirety of the year.

The Mayan individuals embark on sacred journeys to Machimon and hold steadfast faith in his miraculous healing abilities. Once more, I observed an individual in a state of hypnotic trance. The gentleman oriented himself towards the vicinity of the effigy of Machimon. Before him stood a shaman who recited words from a written document. The individual found himself in a state of hypnotic suspension amidst a backdrop of rhythmic incantations and swirling wisps of smoke.

The historical texts of the ancient civilizations of Babylon, Assyria, Egypt, Greece, and Rome indicate that they employed the techniques of trance and suggestion to facilitate the process of healing.

Franz Anton Mesmer, a German medical practitioner, postulated the existence of an inherent energetic force within the fabric of the universe. He referred to the flow as animal magnetism.

In 1766, Mesmer issued his doctoral thesis titled "De planetarum influxu in corpus humanum" (Concerning the Influence of Celestial Bodies on the

Human Body), wherein he expounded upon the impact of the moon and the planets on both the human physique and disease.

After the occurrence of a scandal, Mesmer relocated to Paris in the year 1778. He acquired a residential unit in a prestigious residential area and set up his medical practice.

Mesmer garnered a considerable following. He provided care to patients on an individual basis as well as in group settings. When interacting with individuals, he would adopt a seated position directly facing the patient, ensuring close proximity by aligning his knees with theirs. While maintaining contact, he would firmly clutch the patient's thumbs in his hands, while directing an unwavering gaze into their eyes. Mesmer employed a series of gestures, carefully traversing his hands from the patients' shoulders down to their arms. A multitude of patients experienced anomalous sensations or exhibited convulsions, which were believed to be instrumental in facilitating the curative process. Mesmer would frequently conclude his therapeutic sessions by performing musical melodies on a glass harmonica.

In due course, Paris became split between individuals who perceived him as a fraud, compelled to escape from Vienna, and those who perceived him as a visionary, having made a momentous breakthrough.

In the year 1784, in the absence of any formal plea from Mesmer, King Louis XVI appointed a commission consisting of four esteemed individuals from the Faculty of Medicine and five distinguished members of the Royal Academy of Sciences, with the objective of conducting a thorough examination into the phenomenon known as animal magnetism. The membership of the commission consisted of Joseph-Ignace Guillotin, a renowned medical practitioner credited with the development of the guillotine, alongside Benjamin Franklin, the esteemed diplomat serving as the American ambassador.

The commission conducted a series of experiments with the objective of ascertaining not the effectiveness of

Mesmer's treatment, but rather the discovery of a novel physical fluid. The commission arrived at the determination that no substantiating evidence was found for the existence of said fluid. The treatment's perceived benefits were solely ascribed to the power of the mind, commonly known as "imagination."

In the year of 1843, the esteemed Scottish physician, James Braid introduced the term 'hypnosis' to designate the technique, which had its origins in the practice of animal magnetism. The term originates from the appellation Hypnos, which pertains to the Hellenic deity of slumber.

Development of Self-Hypnosis

In contemporary history, an eminent French psychotherapist and pharmacist named Emile Coue, who was born in 1857, devised a method of psychological healing called autosuggestion.

Autosuggestion constitutes a modality of self-induced hypnotic therapy. Based on Coue's technique, individuals are able to achieve healing by continuously affirming statements like:

Each passing day, I am improving and progressing in every aspect.

From approximately 1900 until Coue's demise in 1926, his methodology experienced considerable renown in both the United Kingdom and the United States.

An alternate method of self-healing, known as Autogenics, came into existence in the 1900s under the tutelage of German physician Johannes Schultz.

Autogenic training enables individuals to exert cognitive influence over biological and physiological processes that are commonly categorized as involuntary, including but not limited to skin temperature, muscle tension, blood pressure, and heart rate.

Autogenic training facilitates the induction of a state of relaxation, thereby aiding in the promotion of healing mechanisms and alleviation of psychosomatic disorders.

Subsequently, autogenics evolved into the practice of biofeedback training.

In the context of biofeedback training, individuals are physically linked to a device which assesses a specific physiological reaction, for instance heart rate, and subsequently provides comprehensible feedback of this measurement to the individual.

As an illustration, the apparatus could emit an audible signal for each cardiac contraction or exhibit the heart rate count per minute via a digitized interface. Furthermore, the patient acquires the ability to discern and respond to nuanced internal bodily changes that impact the monitored response system.

Over time, the individual acquires the ability to generate alterations in that system of responses. Put simply, the patient acquires the ability to deliberately reduce their heart rate.

Biofeedback has emerged as an extensively utilized and widely acknowledged methodology to induce relaxation and reduce physiological arousal among individuals suffering from stress-related conditions.

During the 1930s, Edmund Jacobson, an American psychologist, conceptualized a method of inducing relaxation known as progressive relaxation.

Progressive relaxation entails a methodical process of intentionally activating and subsequently releasing various sets of skeletal muscles. Upon engaging in progressive relaxation techniques, individuals develop a heightened awareness of escalating levels of tension. Frequently, individuals possess the capacity to elicit the relaxation response in the midst of their daily tasks, by engaging in the repetition of a cue word such as "calm" within their internal thoughts.

I have conducted thorough research and have dedicated myself to the daily practice of meditation, which serves as an additional relaxation technique.

In the practice of meditation, individuals cultivate a state of relaxation in both their mental faculties and their physical being. There exists a diverse range of meditation techniques, however, they all commence in a uniform manner by assuming a comfortable seated position on either a cushion or a chair.

The individual gradually eases tension within their body while adopting a slow and controlled breathing pattern. Their focus is directed towards a specific sensation, such as the cyclical process of inhaling and exhaling air, or towards visualizing a specific image or object.

Alternatively, an individual may engage in a tranquil environment and engage in the repetitive recitation of a carefully selected word or phrase, known as a mantra, with the purpose of attaining a state characterized by both relaxation and heightened awareness.

Self-hypnosis training brings the practice of meditation to a more advanced level. It induces a state of tranquil Alpha wave activity, resulting in decreased neural frequency, deep bodily relaxation, and a serene mental state.

The key difference is that autosuggestions are given to oneself during self-hypnosis. Self-suggestions can be imparted through oral, symbolic, affective, and visual means.

The objective of self-hypnosis is to instill constructive and advantageous affirmations in the receptive and susceptible subconscious mind during the practice of self-hypnosis.

Bringing The Mind Back To Sobriety

Your cognitive faculties have consistently demonstrated superiority over the influence of nicotine, however, upon willfully engaging in the consumption of prohibited substances, you have inflicted harm upon the aspect of your cognitive faculties that comprehends the necessity of perceiving the act of smoking cigarettes not as a valuable pursuit, but as an intrinsically detrimental activity that poses harm to your physical well-being.

Certainly, the mind, being a manifestation of ethereal energy, eludes direct observation, and consequently, it is solely within the realm of our spiritual essence that true comprehension and knowledge of the mind reside. In order to derive optimal advantages from intelligent mind control, it is imperative that you maintain a state of complete sobriety. The sole means of upholding astute behavior is through lucid deliberation, enabling one to evaluate their conduct in any given circumstance as either commendable or ill-advised - prudent or imprudent.

It is imperative that you possess the ability to decisively decline any elements that you are consciously aware may pose a detriment to your overall well-being. One might encounter a juncture wherein the notion of every individual eventually meeting their demise becomes apparent, leading to the inclination of embracing it and continuing the habit of smoking.

Nonetheless, it is imperative to acknowledge the truly perilous nature of this behavior - it can be aptly described as self-destructive. In such circumstances, it is crucial to comprehend that one's own mind, rather than being an ally, assumes the role of an adversary. The term "Affirmative" holds significant strength, as does the term "Negative."

If you are genuinely committed to cessation, it would be advisable to make a deliberate choice to attain a state of utmost sobriety, characterized by the ability to employ rational thought and discard any self-centered or pessimistic notions. Subsequently, you will discover that it becomes simpler - and more inherent - to consistently maintain complete mastery over your own behavior.

The Power of Words

Language possesses immense potency. Throughout your lifetime, you have employed them consistently, but in order to thrive in this pursuit, it is imperative to augment your comprehension and appreciation of the genuine significance and authority possessed by words. This comprehension holds the power to achieve remarkable feats for you!

In order for words to exert a significant impact on your psyche and existence, the act of deliberate contemplation is imperative. The act of devoting extended durations of contemplation to a specific term or concept is commonly referred to as concentration. Subsequently, you will gain a profound understanding of the efficacy of language, enabling you to cease your detrimental actions and perpetuate your virtuous conduct. Since the secret relies on word association, it ensures that you remain aligned with your self-determined intentions. Ensuring that each word you contemplate and utter carries significance is imperative.

To illustrate this point, consider the case of an individual who desires to cease the habit of smoking. Your physical and mental faculties may have developed a physiological dependence on smoking, but it is important to acknowledge that your essence or inner self remains devoid of such addiction and has never been influenced by it. Your inner essence collaborates with the force of linguistic energy. The evidence of your contemplation of the phrase "I desire to cease smoking" and your subsequent purchase of this literature demonstrates that your mindset is now embracing more constructive thoughts.

You are now required to grant them greater authority or control, surpassing the mere expression of the phrase 'I need a cigarette.' In doing so, you shall achieve true victory!

What is the process for accomplishing this task? I would suggest engaging in introspective moments of solitude, where you can concentrate on the specific words you wish to imbue with heightened energy and influence. Engage in this process of focused attention as frequently as feasible throughout the course of each day.

In contrast to prevailing notions, it is not necessary to confine oneself to seclusion in order to engage in meditation or concentrate on any desired concept, irrespective of temporal conditions. You are the sole occupant of your mental realm. And irrespective of your surroundings, even in the largest gathering, it is inconsequential. You may even find yourself amidst a group of persistent smokers who engage in the act of lighting up and deriving pleasure from the detriment they inflict upon their own health.

You will enjoy tranquility, as you actively adopt an alternative perspective and understanding of the inherent nature of cigarette smoking.

As you observe your thoughts and the language they employ to encourage you to engage in smoking, it is crucial to identify and eliminate that sequence of words from your mind. Subsequently, it is important to substitute it with its complete contradiction, which should serve as the primary justification for refraining from smoking that cigarette.

For instance, suppose you are encountering challenges at present and contemplating: "I have an absolute need for a cigarette." Another one will not cause harm to me."

This presence within your psyche is characterized by imperfections and harmful consequences. One's immediate inclination should be to adopt a tranquil disposition and confront that thought and sentiment by counteracting it with an antithetical notion, such as, "It is truly unnecessary for me to indulge in a cigarette." An additional occurrence could prove fatal, and you persistently remind yourself of this until reason prevails.

It will not consistently remain challenging as long as you possess a genuine desire to discontinue.

Through engaging in this exercise, you are summoning the potential of your mind, asserting command over your mental faculties, thereby facilitating the generation of beneficial hormones that will inevitably lead to a reduction in the intensity and frequency of these cravings. Here is the proper method for developing a disciplined mindset. You are under no obligation to disclose your actions to anyone.

Now, viewed from your revised standpoint, it becomes evident how receiving a cigarette when offered by a companion bears resemblance to ingesting venom from them. You attain a level of sobriety where you become cognizant of the perilous situation at hand, along with the realization that your companion's actions stem from a lack of knowledge, whether deliberate or inadvertent.

When we are unwell, it becomes necessary to seek the expertise of a medical practitioner. Nevertheless, the act of smoking does not qualify as an organic ailment, thus necessitating an alternative strategy to eliminate this habit. Word-energy is an infallible and reliable method to stimulate the intellect, ensuring a risk-free and effective approach.

Medical professionals, therapists, and specialists in self-improvement unanimously uphold the notion that the key to overcoming addiction lies not in pharmaceutical interventions or therapeutic treatments, but rather within the inherent capabilities of one's own cognitive faculties.

Are you referring to symptoms of nicotine withdrawal? All of these aspects are encompassed within a common framework. The physical form is susceptible to the influence of the mind. Initiate the practice of redirecting your attention towards alternative, more fruitful pursuits and areas of interest.

Now, it is time for you to embark on the journey of self-guided exploration of the essence of words and their personal significance, either through contemplation in solitude or engaging in meaningful discussions with others. Convene a meeting and acquaint yourself with the invaluable knowledge you have acquired, then endeavor to achieve a resolution through diligent application of effort and harnessing your inherent confidence in your actions.

Mind control can only be exerted in a state of sobriety, where one can engage in logical thinking. Therefore, it is imperative to exercise restraint and align one's actions with the fundamental principles of logic. From this line of reasoning, it becomes evident how power operates to ensure a transformative impact on you, without incurring any financial expenditure.

Why would you desire any alternative method, unless it involved exerting complete control over your own thoughts? And bear in mind: you will never be required to utter a single word to individuals. Ah, splendid! Authority successfully reinstated. I hereby declare victory, for the game is over.

This is the opportune time to establish a connection. It concerns the level of control that your mind exerts over your physical being.

As an individual who engages in smoking, you did not connect with this notion, as the inner essence within you engaged in extensive wandering. It is conceivable that you consumed an excessive amount of alcoholic beverages, indulged in nocturnal activities for an extended period while heavily smoking, and potentially utilized profanity without justifiable cause. Your cognitive equilibrium has been disrupted, resulting in diminished concentration, discernment in linguistic expression, and logical reasoning.

Your demeanor has evolved to display a lack of discernment and empathy, which has enabled your thoughts to embrace a growing pessimism, thereby clouding your ability to make sound judgments, exercise prudence, and prioritize matters that have a direct impact on your overall well-being. By neglecting to exercise thoughtfulness in these aspects, you ultimately suffer a loss, thus emphasizing the necessity of maintaining meticulous control over matters that pertain to you.

Considering the multitude of detrimental effects commonly associated with smoking, it can be suggested that had you exercised cognitive control, you would have refrained from initiating this habit. Rational judgment would have superseded any inclination to engage in such a foolish activity.

If you perceive my words as offensive, it suggests that your mindset is inadvertently reinforcing your dependence on smoking, rather than actively seeking methods to overcome it. I am providing guidance on cultivating a mindset shift and training your cognitive processes. In order to overcome addiction, it is imperative for you to develop a strong aversion towards your previous thoughts and behaviors. Failure to do so will result in remaining in a state of vulnerability and submissiveness to nicotine.

Rationality and logical deduction dictate that smoking is inherently unnatural and unwise.

Promoting the Psychological Well-being of Individuals Who Smoke

The practice of smoking is well-known for its ability to numb one's sensitivity. You frequently demonstrate a lack of consideration or appreciation for individuals who do not smoke. While it is not applicable to every individual who engages in smoking, there is a substantial body of statistics indicating that a majority experience the aforementioned consequences. Frequently, individuals who smoke do not have the intention of being inconsiderate, yet this behavior arises as a consequence of cognitive dissonance.

Upon engaging with the concept of consciousness that I have previously elucidated, you will find that your cognitive faculties will be enhanced in such a way that you can perceive the impact that non-smokers in your personal and professional spheres have endured. Those individuals will unquestionably experience great delight (as well as your physical well-being) regarding your undertaking to achieve recovery and progress in abstaining from smoking.

Individuals who have effectively ceased their smoking habit consistently express the liberating experience of no longer being beholden to the vice of tobacco.

Additionally, the ability to overcome the inherent bias towards smokers is a factor that you will undoubtedly find valuable. The cognitive state of individuals who smoke frequently exhibits an irrational inclination towards relinquishing the habit. Rationalizations for smoking can be expediently formulated, such as employing statements like: "The possibility of unforeseen accidents exists, and my demise could occur imminently," or "Mortality is inevitable, and it is inevitable that we succumb to some ailment," or "Indulging in smoking serves as my illicit source of pleasure," or "I restrict my smoking activities solely to outdoor spaces," or "Instances of non-smokers suffering from lung cancer are frequently observed." Kindly supplement your self-justification if desired.

However, as one's mind becomes clear and rationalizes, one may contemplate:

"What have I truly gained from indulging in smoking during these preceding {fill in the blank} years?"

Your thought process may lead you to the conclusion of "enjoyment." This could be because you derive pleasure from smoking after a meal, after engaging in sexual activity, or before going to sleep. It is also possible that you find comfort in the habit of smoking throughout the day or as you wake up in the morning. Due to the fact that it developed into an exceedingly valuable practice.

However, what was the true significance of that delightful practice? After sustained cultivation of affirmative linguistic energy, the solution ought to become conspicuously evident.

Your mental faculties conjured a potent fabrication, as it held no intrinsic worth to you, akin to possessing a cavity in your cranium.

Lorenzo Walden – An Inspiring Tale of Personal Triumph and Achievement!

Allow me to introduce you to my esteemed acquaintance, Lorenzo Walden." In the past, we used to attend religious services together several years ago. Upon our acquaintance, it was evident that both of us adhered to the Christian faith. I will recount to you his experience with smoking.

Between the years of 1981 to 1982, I was employed in a department of the Lindsey Lumber establishment in

Lauderhill, Florida, which served as a preferred shopping destination for Lorenzo and his family. Prior to our acquaintance, two female individuals arrived at the establishment, one of whom was identified as his spouse. We engaged in a highly enjoyable conversation, and approximately two to three weeks subsequently, Lorenzo made his appearance at the establishment.

Before long, Mr. Lorenzo and I engaged in conversation regarding our mutual religious beliefs. The discussion was truly pleasant and characterized by a remarkable sense of harmony, establishing an immediate rapport. During our interaction, my newfound companion Lorenzo experienced immense joy, leading him to engage in playful hops and elegant strides along the aisle of the store.

Consequently, Christian and I both exuded a palpable sense of enthusiasm, and I discerned a genuine sincerity emanating from him. We were in agreement and I felt at ease expressing rational thoughts to him.

Subsequently, Lorenzo unveiled his habit of smoking, which proved to be incompatible with the cultural norms of my homeland in Jamaica. Smoking is strictly prohibited and regarded as a transgression against religious values, with no room for leniency. Immediately, I proceeded to formally accuse the spiritual sibling based on the scriptural allegation of smoking. I artfully and delicately posited my persuasive argument, a task made effortless by the strong rapport we had established.

Initially, I posed an inquiry intended to delve deeper into the matter at hand: "Do you engage in smoking?" I inquired.

And Lorenzo replied: "Yes. My church permits it."

Now, assuming that you are adequately prepared, you will find great delight in the forthcoming segment, as it impeccably showcases the potency of linguistic energy. Consequently, you have the opportunity to imitate and comprehend the cause and effect relationships through the utilization of your own mental directives, scrutiny, and deductions.

I inquired of Lorenzo, "Are you familiar with the scripture passage that states, 'He whom the Son sets free is truly free?'"

"Certainly, I do," Lorenzo affirmed.

I inquired further, questioning his perspective on whether "smoking" can be considered a manifestation of liberty or rather a condition of enslavement.

Upon careful reflection, Lorenzo posited, "I believe it is a form of captivity."

I expressed my agreement by stating, "Indeed... I concur".

Lorenzo witnessed and comprehended the reasoning I presented, cognizant of the logical approach I took, and realized that this very day would signify the culmination of a fifteen-year smoking habit! In that precise instant, he made the firm determination to cease smoking.

He informed me that shortly following the aforementioned incident, he encountered a moment wherein he was on the verge of accepting a cigarette. However, as he extended his hand to grasp it, his memory was reinvigorated, instilling within him a profound vigor emanating from his newly regained mental clarity, ultimately enabling him to decline the cigarette.

This incident took place more than thirty years ago, and as I pen these words today, I take great satisfaction in stating that Lorenzo and I remain steadfast companions (despite no longer adhering to the Christian faith), and he has abstained from smoking since that time.

While I am engaged in composing this message, I am aware that you too have the potential to experience the same.

Extracting Lessons From Prior Endeavors

It has been asserted that the act of cessation is not devoid of difficulty.

Quitting smoking can be an arduous task as many individuals make numerous attempts, mainly due to the highly addictive nature of nicotine, which poses a significant challenge to resist. Nonetheless, one should never relinquish their efforts merely due to previous failures.

Recall your prior endeavors to cease - reflecting on the strategies that proved successful and the ones that were not effective.

If one approach proves ineffective, it is advisable to promptly explore alternative methods without any hesitation. It is highly probable that you can acquire new knowledge with each endeavor.

Considering the present circumstances, it is plausible that this could indeed be the opportune moment for you to permanently cease your engagement.

Obstacles to Smoking Cessation

Many individuals persist in smoking due to the perception that it provides some form of assistance or out of trepidation regarding potential adverse effects following cessation. The following are some of the most prevalent concerns:

The necessity of smoking to alleviate stress can be addressed utilizing numerous alternative methods that are advantageous to the overall well-being of your body, such as engaging in meditation and exercise.

The apprehension of experiencing depression - Cessation of smoking commonly engenders a significant improvement in an individual's self-perception and feeling of complete autonomy. In the event of individuals afflicted with mental illness or those who have previously endured mental health conditions, there are specialized forms of assistance accessible.

The apprehension associated with weight gain - The optimal approach entails directing one's attention towards physical appearance and wellbeing, as opposed to fixating on numerical weight.

There are various alternative approaches at your disposal to assist in the maintenance of your body weight.

The apprehension of withdrawal - It is widely recognized that nicotine functions as an addictive substance, eliciting unpleasant effects upon cessation. However, it is important to note that these symptoms are transient in nature and discontinuing the use of medications will mitigate their impacts.

Make Adequate Preparations and Modify Established Patterns

After gaining knowledge from your prior endeavors, it is crucial that you adequately equip yourself for the imminent eventuality when you intend to permanently terminate the undertaking. Take into account your surroundings and the aspects that require modification. Please remove all tobacco products from your home, vehicle, and place of work, including items such as ashtrays.

Do not permit individuals to smoke in your presence. Kindly request their cooperation in refraining from the use of tobacco in your vicinity or placing cigarettes and other tobacco items where they are within your sight.

If you have previously endeavored to cease this behavior but fell short, I recommend altering your customary patterns. Utilize an entirely alternative route when commuting to the workplace. Please enjoy your morning meal in a different location. Engage in activities that help alleviate your stress.

You may also seek to engage in alternative activities or divert your attention whenever you experience the inclination to utilize tobacco or engage in smoking. Engage in conversation with peers, take a leisurely walk, peruse a literary work, or partake in physical activity. Formulate activities that you can derive pleasure from on a daily basis.

Establishing A Consistent Respiratory Routine

Make an endeavor to integrate a preferred breathing exercise into your daily regimen for a duration of 5 to 10 minutes each day, if feasible. In a formal tone, another way to express the same idea could be: "In lieu of this, you may choose to increase the frequency of the aforementioned procedure at regular intervals throughout the day, particularly upon experiencing an initial indication of distressing withdrawal symptoms." Utilizing the technique of deep breathing, for instance, can serve as an efficient coping mechanism that can be employed whenever an inclination for a cigarette arises.

It is highly probable that you will observe a decrease in the intensity of your need for the item, either upon completion of your deep breathing exercise or shortly thereafter.

The act of engaging in deep breathing exercises may also produce an instantaneous impact, particularly for individuals who are new to this practice. You may have observed a decrease in muscular tension, a relaxation of the shoulders, as well as the release of tension in the jaw. Please take note of your initial emotional state prior to commencing the breathing exercise, as well as your subsequent emotional state upon completion of the breathing exercise.

One option you can consider is keeping a journal or making mental notes about the benefits you receive from each practice.

Do not fret if you do not immediately observe any alterations; this is entirely within the realm of normalcy. Consequently, it might be imperative to monitor your emotions over an extended period to identify alterations in your emotional state.

Ensuring The Continuation Of An Environment Free From Smoketo

In order to mitigate certain manifestations associated with nicotine withdrawal, it is strongly advised to engage in deep breathing exercises. It might be advantageous to integrate a few alternative approaches for maintaining a smoke-free lifestyle into your daily regimen. The subsequent examples enumerated below pertain to such items:

Participating in a support group can effectively foster accountability and reduce stress levels by providing a platform to share experiences with fellow individuals who have either successfully quit smoking or are presently endeavoring to do so.

Counseling Services: In order to support your endeavor to cease smoking, a team of medical practitioners, nursing staff, and other healthcare experts are at your disposal to offer guidance and aid.

To initiate a phone call to a quit-line, one must be aware that smoking cessation services are accessible nationwide, encompassing all states, including the District of Columbia. You have the opportunity to avail complimentary assistance for smoking cessation by dialing a toll-free contact number.

Integrating a smoking cessation application into your daily regimen:

Certain smoking cessation applications deliver constructive affirmations to sustain your motivation as you progress on your tobacco quitting endeavor.

If you are finding it challenging to maintain a smoke-free lifestyle, your physician has the option to prescribe medication to aid in smoking cessation, such as bupropion (sold as Zyban) or naltrexone (sold as Chantix). Additionally, varenicline can be recommended to assist in maintaining a smoke-free status. They may also offer nicotine replacement therapy (NRT), which entails the administration of controlled doses of nicotine devoid of the detrimental substances found in cigarettes, to aid you in gradually transitioning away from your nicotine addiction and abstaining from smoking. NRT is readily accessible in various formulations such as lozenges, patches, gum, and additional options, in addition to being obtainable through prescription medications. It possesses the potential to effectively mitigate the symptoms associated with nicotine withdrawal.

It is advisable to communicate your intention of quitting smoking entirely to your family and friends, even if you have not previously disclosed this to them. Individuals in your social circle who exhibit a strong inclination to support your recent lifestyle change can have a profound impact on your success in relinquishing smoking and prevent regression into prior behaviors.

WHY YOU BEGAN SMOKING

According to the statistical data, a substantial proportion of individuals at the age of 18 initiate the habit of smoking. What could be the attributable factor for this situation? Is this solely attributable to televised advertising, or is their environment exerting an influence? Does society exert any form of pressure? This chapter aims to provide you with solutions to these inquiries and assist you in deliberating on effective strategies for permanently quitting and eliminating your lighter usage.

SEEING IS BELIEVING

A significant portion of the global population relies heavily on advertisements disseminated through television, radio, print media (newspapers and magazines), the internet, and various similar mediums. On your television, you occasionally come across a couple of advertisements pertaining to weight loss equipment. Upon reviewing the advertisement, you determine which product to purchase. Imagine you are on the verge of acquiring a motorcycle. You peruse a selection of magazines and select your preferred choice. Similarly, advertisements pertaining to cigarettes from diverse origins possess the potential to shape one's thought processes regarding smoking. Upon witnessing these advertisements, a significant number of individuals who have not yet smoked develop contemplations regarding partaking in their initial inhalation. Additionally, individuals who engage in smoking and express a desire to cease this habit may experience a dilution of their resolve upon encountering these advertisements.

ULTIMATE STRESS BUSTER!

Nicotine is widely regarded as a highly effective means of alleviating stress among numerous individuals. Throughout history, smoking has been employed by soldiers as a method to manage the stress imposed by war. Accordingly, they resort to cigarette consumption as a means of self-medication. Individuals experiencing significantly less severe levels of stress have also been observed to commence smoking in order to cope with the feelings of anxiety and apprehension associated with their unique circumstances. Regrettably, this pattern persists and they develop into individuals who continuously engage in smoking.

DID THEY GET YOU? ARE THEY STILL...?

The media assumes a comparable role (in relation to advertisements) within the decision-making process of an individual with regards to whether or not to engage in smoking. Similar to how the apparel trends of actors in a television series or films have an impact on individuals, the act of smoking by these actors has the potential to influence others. They may perceive smoking as a means to enhance their social image among peers and professional acquaintances. Despite the efforts of antismoking organizations to diminish the portrayal of smoking onscreen in recent years, it takes merely a brief moment for certain individuals to assimilate such detrimental behaviors.

Excellent, so you do not require the assistance of a physician?

The majority of individuals who partake in smoking assert that they experience a euphoric sensation subsequent to each instance of smoking. Additionally, they assert that this sensation exerts a direct impact on their levels of stress or appetite. Additionally, numerous individuals who engage in smoking express that it serves as a commendable method of self-medicating symptoms associated with conditions that impact their stress levels and physical discomfort. Individuals afflicted with mental disorders such as depression or anxiety may resort to smoking as a coping mechanism to alleviate certain manifestations. However, the reality is that this self-medication is only a temporary measure. The utilization of smoking may alleviate these symptoms to a considerable extent; however, it is invariably accompanied by numerous detrimental side effects that will be explored in subsequent sections.

Your understanding of the matter is completely incorrect.

In addition to the advertisements highlighting the adverse health consequences of smoking, there are situations where tobacco is promoted as a means of enhancing vitality and well-being. Likewise, the enduring misconception that tobacco enhances virility is upheld in the United States through advertisements of yore, exemplified by iconic figures like the Marlboro Man who were portrayed as epitomes of masculinity. Furthermore, according to certain myths, the consumption of "light" cigarettes is believed to be less detrimental than that of other variants. Hence, such myths can effectively steer smokers towards adopting safer cigarette alternatives, without necessarily considering the prospect of quitting altogether.

It is permissible to hold them responsible.

Juveniles acquire knowledge and behaviors through observation of their immediate environment. In the event that either or both parents engage in smoking, it is highly likely that the offspring will similarly acquire the habit at some point in their life. It is inaccurate to assert that there is absolutely no possibility for a child with non-smoker parents to grow up as a non-smoker; there exist numerous factors that could potentially contribute to their initiation of smoking. It is incumbent upon parents to discourage the endorsement of smoking as a lethal habit and to dissuade their children from its adoption.

HA, THEY LOVE ME!

Social incentives, the gratification individuals experience when engaging in communal pursuits, are a prominent driving force behind the development and persistence of smoking dependencies. Individuals desire a feeling of connectedness and inclusion. They seek to align themselves with and be beloved by a discernible collective, owing to their perception of impressive qualities.

Curiously, a substantial number of individuals who engage in smoking tend to have closest companions who also partake in the habit.

I possess a propensity for taking risks.

Certain individuals possess a propensity for exhibiting a borderline disposition, deriving satisfaction from engaging in precarious conduct. Among those individuals who possess a propensity for risk-taking, some derive satisfaction from their ability to discreetly indulge in smoking within designated non-smoking zones.

A significant proportion of the contemporary youth possess an inclination towards defying societal norms, as they harbour an aversion towards abiding by regulations and constraints, thereby deliberately assuming a contrarian stance to contradict the guidance imparted by their elders and predecessors.

In spite of the stringent regulations imposed by government authorities regarding the acquisition and trade of these tobacco commodities, a considerable number of individuals choose to contravene them, deriving a sense of personal satisfaction from this defiance. They derive immense gratification from transgressing norms and accessing, as well as utilizing, these prohibited goods intended for individuals beyond their age.

Natural Ways To Quit

At present, it is highly probable that you are adequately poised to permanently cease your cigarette consumption. It is likely that you have made previous attempts to cease given the various alternatives available. Similar to most individuals, you find yourself repeatedly drawn to that "familiar companion," the cigarette.

Create a comprehensive inventory of food varieties that can be effectively kept within your household, serving as a favorable "substitute" for satiating cravings when they arise anew. Please ensure that this checklist is readily accessible and consistently verify that your refrigerator or cabinets are adequately supplied. Your listing may encompass the following components:.

By exploring these innovative options, you can tantalize your taste buds while maintaining your well-being.

It is imperative that you resist the temptation to compensate for this deficiency by adding salt and other undesirable components to your meals. Instead, endeavor to prepare some recipes that are exceptionally hot and spicy, or that possess novelty and distinctiveness.

Engage in the exploration of novel culinary experiences.

The cost in both dollars and cents.

Furthermore, this hydration aids in expeditiously eliminating toxins from your system. As previously mentioned, the toxins and chemicals responsible for your craving for cigarettes are still present in your system even after you have quit smoking. Therefore, consuming adequate amounts of water will expedite the process of eliminating these harmful substances and help regulate your cravings.

One of the reasons why it is exceedingly challenging to cease the habit of smoking cigarettes is due to its physical nature, which renders it immensely resistant to cessation. When it comes to smoking cigarettes, one must recognize the immense difficulty of breaking a deeply ingrained physical habit. Please honestly communicate to them about your efforts to cease smoking, as well as the significant challenges posed by being in the presence of individuals who engage in smoking. By exercising caution in the selection of your diet and indulgences, not only will you avert the risk of undesirable weight gain, but you will also experience an overall sense of well-being. This will undoubtedly serve as a catalyst to sustain your commitment towards maintaining a newfound healthy lifestyle void of smoking.

The Psychological and Cognitive Aspects of Smoking Cessation.

The act of smoking cigarettes is not merely a physical craving; it is an experience that any individual who indulges in smoking will readily acknowledge. It serves as somewhat of a means to alleviate tension. It seems to provide a sense of relaxation and rejuvenation.

When an individual fails to acquire proficient problem-solving skills to address their stress and concerns and resorts to tobacco to alleviate them, they subsequently confront the double predicament of not only grappling with these anxieties upon cessation, but also grappling with their unrelenting cravings, which only exacerbate their restlessness.

Moreover, a significant number of individuals who initiate cigarette smoking during their time in educational institutions do so with the intention of being perceived as "trendy" or fitting in with a specific social group. As previously alluded to, it is unfortunate that such perceptions prevail, as many individuals believe that smoking enhances their image, portrays them as resilient, or garners respect from their peers.

How does one successfully overcome the strong grip that cigarettes maintain over them?

There exists a scientific foundation that supports the notion that smoking cigarettes induces a state of mental and physical relaxation. Nicotine in its pure form exerts a literal influence on an individual, and it is verifiable that engaging in manual tasks reduces the likelihood of experiencing distress. The human body expels stress through the process of perspiration during the completion of tasks.

If you are perusing this publication, it is deduced that you have already expressed your belief in the significance of health and good practices. Consequently, it might be opportune to consider how this belief manifests in your personal conduct. Whom do you currently admire, the individual who indulges in idle daydreaming while unemployed, or the individual who exerts effort and possesses a strong level of fitness and vitality?

Make a checklist.

By comprehending all the factors that currently entitle you to prestige and foster a strong self-perception, there should be no need for you to rely upon frivolous trends endorsed by ignorant individuals, or on what you believed to be magnificent during your youth and inexperience.

If one's motivation for smoking is driven by a desire to appear impressive or tough, it may be prudent to reassess such priorities.

Exercising emotional control while ceasing an activity.

You may need to provide some challenging and swift insight to your acquaintances at present. Once more, a genuine close companion is an individual who supports and respects you and your choices. In the event that you have companions who engage in smoking, it is possible that they themselves are not ready to quit. Nevertheless, one ought to consider their response towards your decision. If their encouragement to persist in the habit of smoking cigarettes is motivated by a desire to avoid exclusion or guilt regarding their own decision to continue smoking, can they genuinely be considered a true companion?

Aiming to look amazing.

Inquire independently about your thoughts regarding individuals, relationships, life goals, and your perceived priorities during your time in school. Engaging in late-night activities may have been a regular occurrence; it is likely that you now prioritize getting a sufficient night's sleep in order to arrive at work punctually.

It pertains to the act of smoking cigarettes. Upon what basis do you form the assumption that individuals are inherently exceptional or desirable acquaintances in the present era? What type of personality do you hold in high regard?

At this present moment, it could be deemed a prudent recommendation to compile a comprehensive inventory comprising all the factors that bring about satisfaction and contribute towards one's personal excellence and resilience. The priority on your agenda should be the intention to cease the habit of smoking. Are you able to regulate your emotions or abstain from engaging in gossip about other individuals?

Participating in smoking may have conferred membership into the esteemed "in" circle or evoked admiration for your perceived bravery during your youth; however, I encourage you to ponder this matter earnestly as a mature individual. There is decidedly no aspect of wonder when it comes to cancer cells, the condition of being confined to an iron lung, the inability to laugh without expelling fragments of the lungs, and the impact of making those in close proximity unwell.

If you have indeed resorted to smoking as a means to alleviate stress, boredom, tension, or any other adverse emotions, it is imperative to confront these issues directly and acquire alternative, healthier methods of coping. Below are some ideas:

Typically, the initial week poses the greatest challenges, thus it is advisable to undertake small tasks daily. Upon successfully completing your first entire day without smoking, treat yourself to a copy of your favorite published material. Subsequently, individuals may opt to rent a video, among other possible options.

Whilst you have your pen and paper at hand, we kindly suggest that you compile a comprehensive list enumerating the various methods through which you may reward yourself. We kindly remind you to include cost-effective options, as well as those that may be somewhat more extravagant in nature. Correlate these goals with your intentions for quitting smoking.

Furthermore, it would be advantageous to consider alternative strategies for effectively addressing your anxiety. One such approach involves directly managing the situation rather than solely attempting to suppress your emotions. In the event that both you and your partner are experiencing significant difficulties, it may be appropriate to seek the assistance of a professional marriage counselor. If you are truly overwhelmed by your obligations in the workspace, it is advisable to have open and sincere communication with your manager or supervisor. Additionally, express your concern for the well-being of the company and the clients, rather than solely emphasizing your personal comfort.

Make a checklist.

Alternative ways to manage stress could involve reaching out to your acquaintances and engaging in open conversation about your current concerns, or seeking assistance from a trustworthy individual. Do you have access to a collegiate counselor who can provide support during examinations, or a trusted elder family member who reliably offers valuable guidance?

Renouncing the habit of cigarette smoking is arguably one of the most arduous undertakings that individuals have endeavored or will ever undertake. Numerous individuals assert that giving up smoking has proven to be more challenging for them in comparison to discontinuing illicit substances.

Following your evening meal, you will proceed to embark on a leisurely promenade, engage in social interaction by contacting a close acquaintance, peruse a few online chapters of your preferred literary work, or partake in a relaxing immersion within a heated bath. While proceeding towards your destination, you can utilize this period to mentally prepare yourself for the day ahead. By being better prepared, you are likely to experience reduced stress levels.

What specific stress-reducing activities do you enjoy or have an interest in exploring? How about incorporating yoga or meditation into one's routine? May I ask about the particular leisure activities that you may have neglected but previously enjoyed, such as painting, reading, knitting, needlepoint, woodworking, automotive mechanics, architectural design, scrapbooking, jewelry making, and the like?

After abstaining from cigarette smoking for a few weeks, treat yourself to a prolonged session of massage therapy. After the passage of one month, obtain for yourself that recently-released coat that has captured your attention.

Let us examine some of these here.

Alternatively, you are proceeding directly to the workplace and have a brief period of time while driving before your arrival. You have apprehensions related to your work, much like most individuals do, and typically indulge in a cigarette during the commute. Currently exactly what?

Challenging circumstances have become an integral aspect of our contemporary existence, affecting virtually everyone, making it crucial to recognize that you are not alone in experiencing these situations, for they are by no means unusual occurrences.

Having finished your evening meal, you are now inexplicably overwhelmed by fatigue resulting from your rigorous labor at the workplace or the demands of caring for your children. Typically, it is customary to ignite a cigarette as you allocate a few moments to unwind.

Considering your desire to relinquish, what specific course of action do you intend to pursue?

When achieving success in your program, it is imperative to grant yourself certain rewards throughout the journey, in order to serve as reminders of your accomplishments and to serve as incentives for your continued progress.

In order to assist you in this regard, the first step you can take is to mentally equip yourself for challenging situations. Several individuals who frequently take tests often experience a profound sense of isolation, believing that they are the sole individuals grappling with these challenges. In contrast, they perceive others' marriages as flawless and assume that everyone else effortlessly handles their workload in the professional sphere.

Award on your own.

Improving state of mind.

www.ingramcontent.com/pod-product-compliance
Lightning Source LLC
Chambersburg PA
CBHW050358120526
44590CB00015B/1731